Canadian Structures

STADIUMS

TRUE NORTH

BY TAMMY GAGNE

True North is published by Beech Street Books
27 Stewart Rd. Collingwood, ON Canada L9Y 4M7

www.beechstreetbooks.ca

Produced by Red Line Editorial

Photographs ©: Adam Melnyk/Shutterstock Images, cover, 1; Public Domain, 4–5; VIEW Pictures Ltd/Alamy, 7; Red Line Editorial, 8, 9; Adwo/Shutterstock Images, 10–11; meunierd/Shutterstock Images, 13; Design Pics/Thinkstock, 14–15; Volodymyr Kyrylyuk/Shutterstock Images, 16–17; Leszek Wrona/Dreamstime, 18; Songquan Deng/Shutterstock Images, 20–21

Editor: Heather C. Hudak
Designer: Laura Polzin

Library and Archives Canada Cataloguing in Publication

Gagne, Tammy, author
    Stadiums / by Tammy Gagne.

(Canadian structures)
Includes bibliographical references and index.
Issued in print and electronic formats.
ISBN 978-1-77308-015-4 (hardback).--ISBN 978-1-77308-043-7 (paperback).--
ISBN 978-1-77308-071-0 (pdf).--ISBN 978-1-77308-099-4 (html)

    1. Stadiums--Canada--Juvenile literature. I. Title.

TH4714.G34 2016   j725'.8270971   C2016-903617-0
                                              C2016-903618-9

Printed in the United States of America
Mankato, MN
August 2016

TABLE OF CONTENTS

TD PLACE

What do professional football games and music concerts have in common? They all take place in stadiums. Some stadiums are simple one-storey arenas. Others have many levels and roofs. Some of these buildings are as interesting as the events they host.

Engineers must think about many details when planning a stadium. First they think about how it will be used. They also think about how many people it must hold. They even think of how the weather might affect it. Strong winds can make tall buildings sway. The building materials must remain strong in all situations.

PURPOSE

TD Place in Ottawa stands on a historic site. In the early 1900s the Ottawa Exposition Grounds were known as Lansdowne Park.

TD Place is home to the Ottawa Redblacks of the Canadian Football League (CFL).

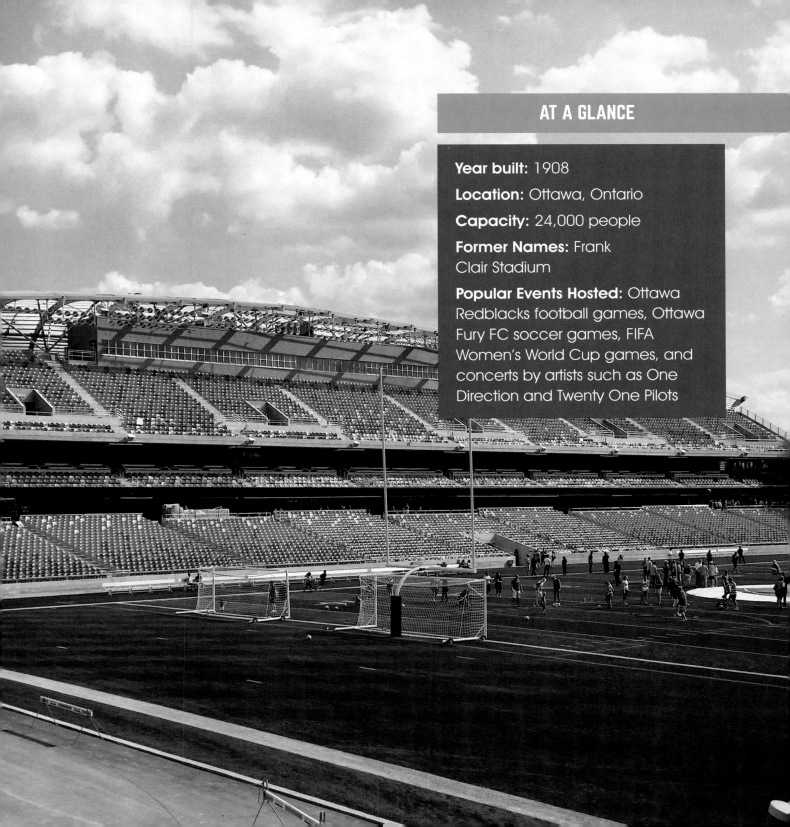

AT A GLANCE

Year built: 1908

Location: Ottawa, Ontario

Capacity: 24,000 people

Former Names: Frank Clair Stadium

Popular Events Hosted: Ottawa Redblacks football games, Ottawa Fury FC soccer games, FIFA Women's World Cup games, and concerts by artists such as One Direction and Twenty One Pilots

People mainly came to the grounds to watch football games. The stadium was the home of the Ottawa Rough Riders from 1908 to 1996.

STRONG & STABLE

From 1966 to 1967 much of the grounds were torn down to make way for a stadium. The structure was built from steel. Steel is strong, cheap, and easy to work with. The steel framework holds up the building. It works much like the skeleton of the human body.

A building needs a **foundation**. Over time the ground moves. Without a foundation the building would move with it. Walls and floors could separate from one another. The earth freezes and thaws. When the ground is soft, a building without a foundation could sink. Most steel-framed buildings have **concrete** foundations to support them. Concrete is adaptable and durable. TD Place's stands are also made out of concrete.

At first the concrete stadium had only one level. The floor rose higher behind each row of seats. A roof over part of the stadium sheltered people from poor weather. In 1975 the bleachers on the south side were rebuilt and expanded upward.

In 2012 a double-deck stand, or second tier, was added on the south side of TD Place. The roof was removed as well. Workers wrapped the south side of the stadium in a wooden **veil**. It is 154 metres wide and nearly 26 metres tall. It looks a bit like giant window blinds.

All of TD Place's wooden surfaces are sloped. This helps keep rainwater from pooling.

The wood for the veil comes from Alaskan yellow cedar trees. It does not need to be treated with chemicals. It naturally resists rot and decay. The veil helps keep the stands shaded. The sun and rain will turn the wood silver over time. The wood comes from the northern Pacific coast region. It was glued together before being shipped to Ottawa.

The veil is made up of 750,000 parts. It has 24 vertical supports. Each one has a unique shape. They give the stadium a curved look. More than 1,800 purlins, or secondary supports, stick out from the vertical supports. They help hold the structure in place. Each one is notched on the end to fit around the vertical supports. Nearly 160,000 kilograms of steel and more than 3,500 bolts were used to make the veil.

FORCES OF NATURE

Different forces act on structures such as stadiums. Engineers need to consider these factors when designing the buildings. Four forces they consider are **gravity**, **tension**, **shear**, and **compression**.

The location of a building's centre of gravity greatly affects how stable the structure is. Gravity is the force that pulls everything to the earth. For a simple structure, the centre of gravity is in the middle of the structure. For a leaning structure, the centre of gravity is not above the middle. This causes gravity to produce a turning effect called a **moment**. It tips the structure over. The taller the structure, the more mass it has above the centre of gravity. It has a more powerful turning force and is more likely to topple. Smart planning and strong

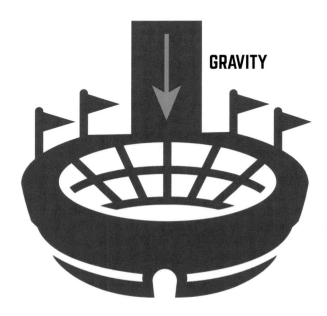

GRAVITY

building materials can make even leaning structures safe. If the moment is small enough, the building materials will hold it together.

Tension and shear create big challenges for stadium roofs. Certain materials do not hold up well to these forces. Tension happens when two forces pull an object in opposite directions. They stretch the object and pull it apart. Shear loading happens when two forces are side by side. They push or pull, sliding an object apart sideways. This causes the object to rip apart.

Compression happens when two forces push toward each other. The forces squeeze the object between them. The more weight a beam needs to support, the more the force of compression acts on it. Forces are pushing on it from above and below.

OLYMPIC STADIUM

Montreal's Olympic Stadium served as the main site for the 1976 Summer Olympic Games. The field and the stands were built in time for the games. But the full structure was not complete. The Canadian government planned to complete the project after the Olympics. But engineers ran into many problems along the way.

Olympic Stadium was to feature a **retractable** roof. During good weather, the roof would be opened to let in warm air and sunshine. During cold or wet weather, it would remain closed. Engineers designed a leaning tower to stand next to the stadium. It would lift and lower the roof.

Many of the problems engineers faced when building Olympic Stadium had to do with the roof.

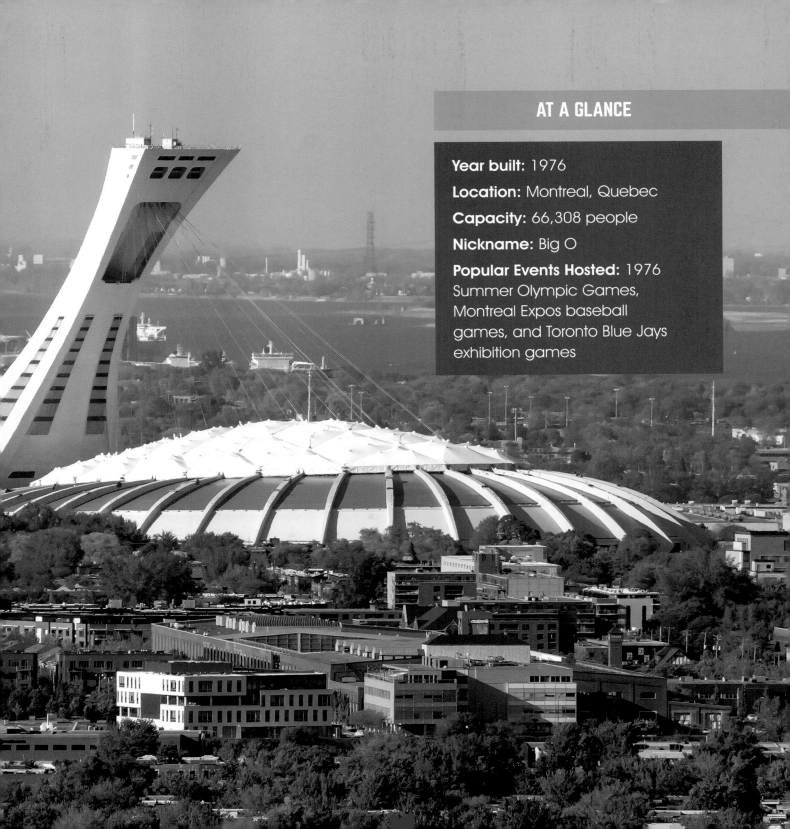

AT A GLANCE

Year built: 1976

Location: Montreal, Quebec

Capacity: 66,308 people

Nickname: Big O

Popular Events Hosted: 1976 Summer Olympic Games, Montreal Expos baseball games, and Toronto Blue Jays exhibition games

STRONG & STABLE

In the 1970s workers began building the tower from concrete. But it was too heavy for the final product. The more the tower leaned forward, the more pressure gravity applied.

To keep the heavy tower from falling over, engineers decided to build a base made of 145,000 tonnes of solid concrete. It was built 10 metres below ground. This helped distribute the weight of the tower. But in 1986 part of the concrete fell off Olympic Stadium's tower during a baseball game. The engineers decided to complete the tower using steel. It is much lighter weight.

By 1988 Olympic Stadium's new tower and roof were complete. Still they had problems. The fabric roof was meant to fold up like an umbrella into the tower. But it took 25 minutes to open the roof. By then the Kevlar material ripped in many places. Kevlar is the strong material used to make bulletproof vests. It is not good at withstanding compression. Snow and ice caused it to rip more over time.

When an object is stretched in opposite directions, it is under the load of tension. This process stresses the object. When two forces pull an object without opposing each other directly, the object is under a shear loading. This can cause the object to tear.

After being closed for many seasons, the roof was replaced in 1998. The new roof did not retract and was made from Teflon-coated fibreglass. This material is strong and sturdy. But there were still structural problems. The fibreglass was not sturdy enough. By 2013 it had more than 3,400 rips.

The total cost to build Olympic Stadium was more than $1 billion.

Today the stadium hosts many sports events, and about 250,000 people visit the tower each year. It is the tallest inclined structure in the world.

Chapter Three

COMMONWEALTH STADIUM

Commonwealth Stadium in Edmonton, Alberta, is the second-largest outdoor sports venue in Canada. It was built to host the 1978 **Commonwealth Games**.

Commonwealth Stadium was upgraded in 2010. Edmonton wanted to host the Grey Cup. But the stadium was in poor shape. It was built mostly from concrete. Water leakage was an issue.

STRONG & STABLE

Workers reinforced damaged areas with steel connection assemblies. Unlike concrete, steel would not break down from the weather. Workers also applied waterproof coatings to the new, stronger joints. These coatings would keep the rain and snow out in the future. Workers used materials that would last a long time. They recycled materials they removed from the structure.

Poor weather caused many problems for the structure of Commonwealth Stadium.

Chapter Four

BC PLACE

BC Place in Vancouver was built to serve as the home of two sports teams. They are the BC Lions and the Vancouver Whitecaps. When it first opened, this stadium was best known for its domed roof. The inflatable Teflon-coated fibreglass roof cost less to build than a rigid one. But operating it was not cheap. Fans were used to keep the air pressure at the right balance. The fans were very large and had to be on all the time. The stadium's power bills were huge. And the roof couldn't support the load of heavy snow in winter. A large snowfall in January 2007 caused it to cave in.

On hot, humid days the indoor stadium was unpleasant. Some events could not be held at the stadium during the hottest months. The stadium's only source of light was indoor

BC Place is on the north side of False Creek in Vancouver.

What types of stadium roofs are strong and stable? What can stadiums do to be more environmentally efficient?

At BC Place only the part of the roof that covers the field retracts.

electric lights. No sunlight could get inside. A **renovation** that began in 2010 changed all this.

STRONG & STABLE

Workers replaced the domed roof with a retractable one. It was made from a special fabric called TENARA. The fabric is **translucent**. It allows natural light inside the stadium. It folds up quickly and without damage. It does not crack or crease.

The roof has 36 air-filled cushions. Each one has two layers of fabric. They can be inflated to hold up under the weight of snow. Sensors check the load on the support cables every four seconds. They report to a computer that can adjust the air pressure as needed. The cushions' double layers form a waterproof seal on the inside edge of the roof. When the roof is open, the cushions deflate. Cables move the fabric from the sides toward the centre of the roof. They are housed inside a pod above the stadium's videoboard. Opening or closing the roof takes just 20 minutes.

BC Place's roof is the largest covering of its kind in the world. The opening measures 100 metres long by 85 metres wide. The roof is very energy efficient. The fabric helps hold warm air in when needed. It lets hot air out when the roof opens. It lowered the cost of heating and cooling the stadium by 25 percent.

During the upgrade the playing field was replaced with all-weather turf. It is synthetic and remains in better shape than real grass would. Better lighting and sound systems were put in place. And 50,000 seats were replaced with newer, more comfortable ones.

The main stadium has reserved platforms for people with mobility challenges. As well, some suites have removable seats to allow for wheelchairs. There is even a dedicated accessible entrance from the parking lot.

Year built: 1983

Location: Vancouver, British Columbia

Capacity: 54,320 people

Popular Events Hosted: BC Lions football games, 2010 Winter Olympic Games, 2010 Paralympics, Vancouver Whitecaps FC soccer games, FIFA Women's World Cup games, and concerts by singers such as Taylor Swift

Chapter Five

ROGERS CENTRE

Toronto's Rogers Centre is one of Canada's most modern stadiums. The outside of the stadium is made of glass and concrete. Glass allows sunlight in while concrete makes the structure strong. Inside, guests are greeted by LED screens displaying a range of 4.3 trillion colours.

STRONG & STABLE

Rogers Centre was the first stadium in the world to have a retractable roof that opens all the way. The roof has four sections made of steel and plastic. Each panel rides along track beams made of reinforced concrete. One panel remains still while the others retract. Two panels slide over the non-moving panel. The third panel slides below it.

Rogers Centre has an arena, health club, hotel, restaurants, and shopping.

Year built: 1989

Location: Toronto, Ontario

Capacity: 10,000 to 66,000 people, depending on the event

Former name: SkyDome

Popular Events Hosted: Toronto Blue Jays baseball games, Toronto Argonauts football games, and concerts by artists such as Justin Bieber and Jason Aldean

GLOSSARY

COMMONWEALTH GAMES
a sporting event that takes place every four years between 71 nations that were once part of the British Empire

COMPRESSION
a pushing force that shortens the object it acts on

CONCRETE
a building material made from a mixture of water, cement, and sand or crushed stone

FOUNDATION
a solid structure on which a tower is built

GRAVITY
a force that pulls things down toward the surface of the earth

MOMENT
a turning force that can cause a structure to topple

RENOVATION
the changing of a structure to improve its condition or function

RETRACTABLE
capable of being opened and closed

SHEAR
a force that pushes on different points of a structure in opposite directions at the same time

TENSION
a pulling force that lengthens the object it acts on

TRANSLUCENT
clear enough to allow light to pass through

VEIL
something that covers or hides something else

TO LEARN MORE

BOOKS

Brain, Marshall. *The Engineering Book*. New York: Sterling, 2015.

Dillon, Patrick. *The Story of Buildings: From the Pyramids to the Sydney Opera House and Beyond*. Somerville, MA: Candlewick, 2014.

Mooney, Carla. *Stadiums and Coliseums*. Vero Beach, FL: Rourke Educational Media, 2015.

WEBSITES

BC PLACE
www.bcplace.com

TD PLACE
www.tdplace.ca

TECHNOLOGY STUDENT
www.technologystudent.com/forcmom/force1.htm

23

INDEX

ABOUT THE AUTHOR

Tammy Gagne has written more than 150 books for adults and children. She lives with her husband and son. One of her favourite pastimes is visiting schools to talk to kids about the writing process.